# Pretty 2 Me

By Keyonna Monroe

Illustrated by Danh Tran

3G Publishing, Inc.
4495 Atlanta Highway, Suite C28
Loganville, GA 30052
www.3gpublishinginc.com



First published by 3G Publishing, Inc., June, 2021.

Printed in the United States of America

ISBN: 9781941247938

# Dedication

This book is dedicated to all the girls in my organization who struggled with self love, acceptance, and questioned their worthiness. To all the beautiful souls that walked into my classroom insecure, and left so loved and empowered that negativity no longer stood a chance. You are and will always be Pretty2Me!!!!

My name is Sophia and I like to read. I wear these things called glasses and they help me to see.

Some say glasses are weird, and they call me a geek. My friends say they are cool, so who cares what they think!

Ms. Monroe says, "What matters the most, is what you believe". Then she gave me a mirror, and I look Pretty2Me!

My name is Yulan, and I just got new braces. When I laugh and I smile people tend to make faces.

I tried colorful bands to make them look cool, but they laughed even more when I showed them at school.

Ms. Monroe says, "The only thing that matters is what you feel and believe." Then she gave me a mirror, and I look Pretty2Me!

My name is Rayne, and I just beat cancer! When I grow up, I am going to be a ballet dancer. Sometimes I get down, because I lost all my hair. What if people don't like me? What if no one ever cares?

Ms. Monroe says, "What matters the most, is what I feel and believe." Then she gave me a mirror, and I was Pretty2Me!

My name is Madison, they call me Maddy instead. I get teased about my dark skin and the hair on my head.

Sometimes I try to hide it, just so that I can fit in. It never really works, and they would just tease me again.

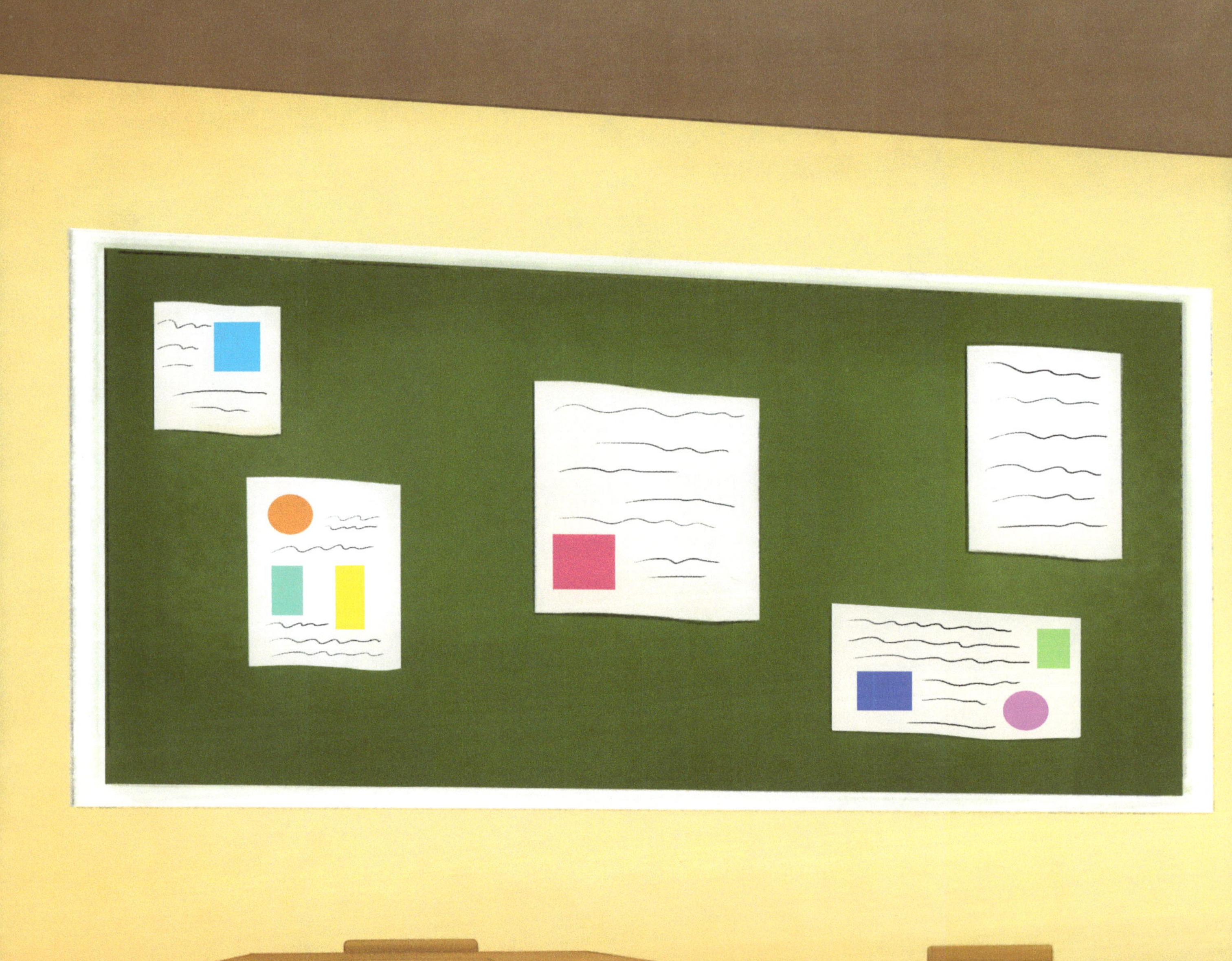

Ms. Monroe said to me, "Believe with your heart, and believe what you see." Then she gave me a mirror, and I was Pretty2Me!

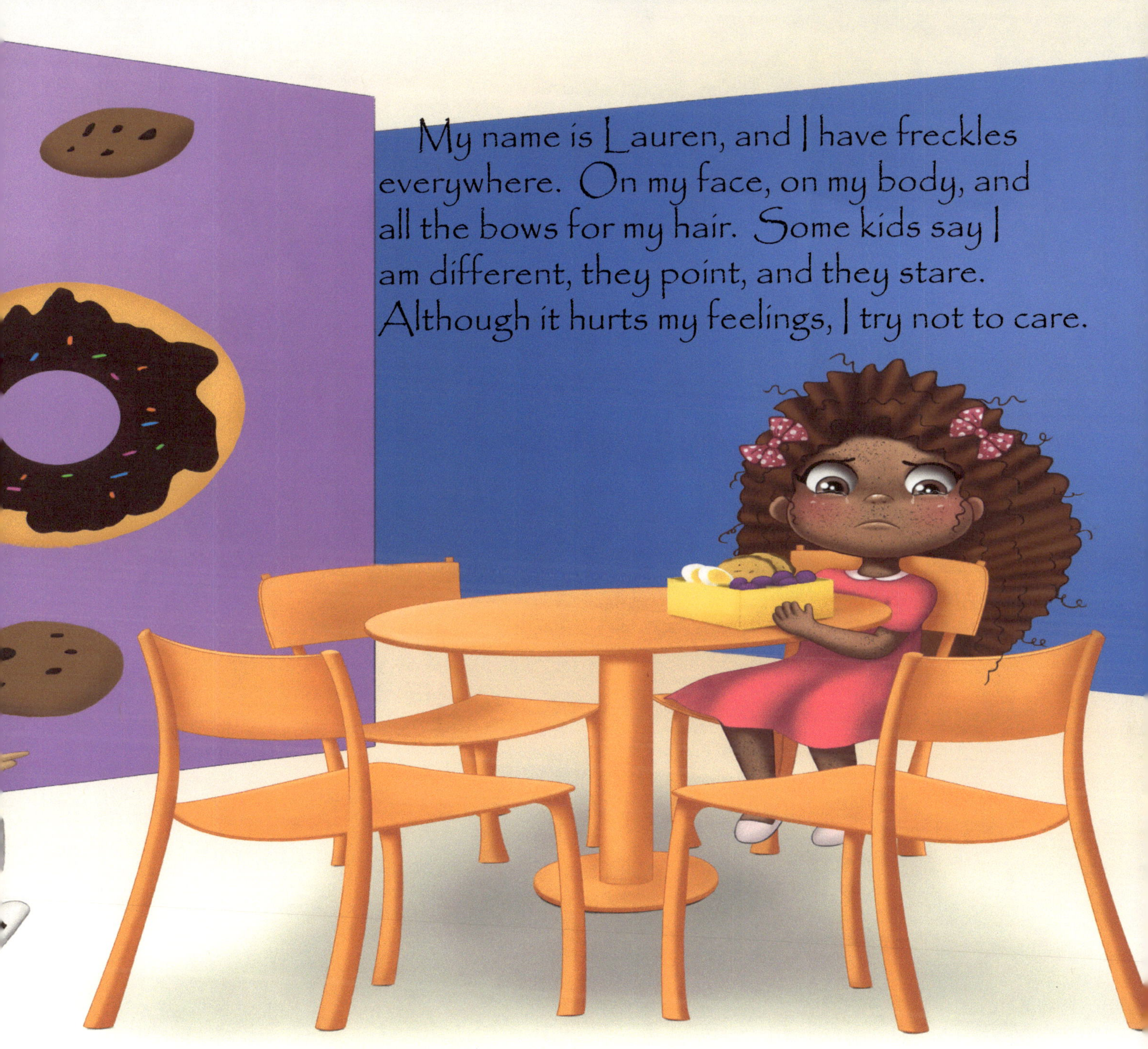

My name is Lauren, and I have freckles everywhere. On my face, on my body, and all the bows for my hair. Some kids say I am different, they point, and they stare. Although it hurts my feelings, I try not to care.

Ms. Monroe reminded me, "Your worth comes from what only you choose to see." Then she handed me a mirror, and I was Pretty2Me!

My name is Sky, and I have vitiligo. It is a skin pigmentation in case you did not know. Some kids say that I am different, and I should cover my skin, and that I will never be pretty in the world we live in.

Ms. Monroe says, "It is for you to choose in what story you believe." Then she handed me a mirror and I was Pretty2Me!

So, the moral of the story is, that beauty starts from inside. If you love who you are, then show it with pride. People have an opinion you do not have to accept. The only opinion that matters is the one you have of yourself.

So, when you step outside the house, and you give the world a view, make sure you step out with confidence knowing that you are beautiful to you!

Self Love is the
Best Love!

# The End

www.ingramcontent.com/pod-product-compliance
Lightning Source LLC
LaVergne TN
LVHW070203110826
845147LV00002B/488

* 9 7 8 1 9 4 1 2 4 7 9 3 8 *